REVERSE COLORING BOOK

YOU DRAW
THE LINES

HOW TO USE THIS BOOK

In a reverse coloring book, the colors are already printed on the page, and your job is to draw lines over the colors to create a new image. Unlike Traditional Coloring Books, Where You Add Colors, into a blank Page, in reverse, Coloring Book, You Get To Create Outlines, patterns, and Shapes on The Top of preexisting Colors. Making beautiful works of art that are true reflections of your own style and personality has never been easier.

Bold lines: Lines that are thick and dark can make a strong visual statement. To draw them, just grab a heavy black pencil or marker.

Fine lines: You can add some visual interest to your coloring page by including some fine lines. To draw them, all you need is a pen, pencil, or marker with a fine point.

Dots and Circles: You may add a sense of motion and rhythm to your coloring page by making circles and dots move in different ways. For example, you could make circles that are concentric, overlapping, or completely random.

Abstract lines: Lines that don't represent anything in the real world are called abstract lines. Adding dimension, texture, or movement to your coloring page is easy if you use abstract lines. Make lines that are diagonal, zigzag, squiggly, or otherwise interesting, and play around with color and line thickness to make something truly one-of-a-kind and visually engaging.

Create your own designs: At Last, The Reverse Coloring Book's Preexisting Colors Can Serve as Inspiration for Your Own Shapes and Designs! You are free to sketch anything that comes to mind, be it a star, a flower, an animal, or anything else. Allow your imagination to run free and come up with a coloring page that no one else has.

swirls

messy or clean
either is a win

shading

crazy lines

play around with
thickness

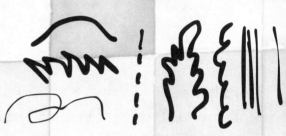

florals

use different
sizes and shapes

shapes

any and all shapes are
easy and effective

double up lines

This Is a fun Meditative Way, To fix Anything
You Think Is a screw-up (but really there are
no screw-ups)

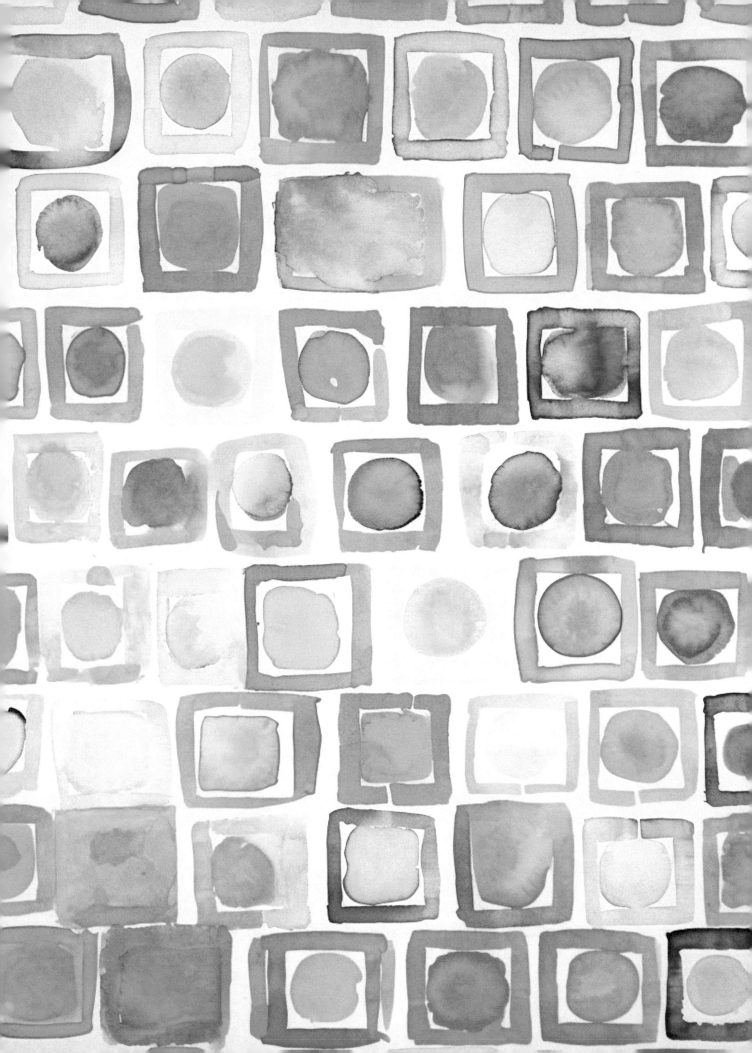

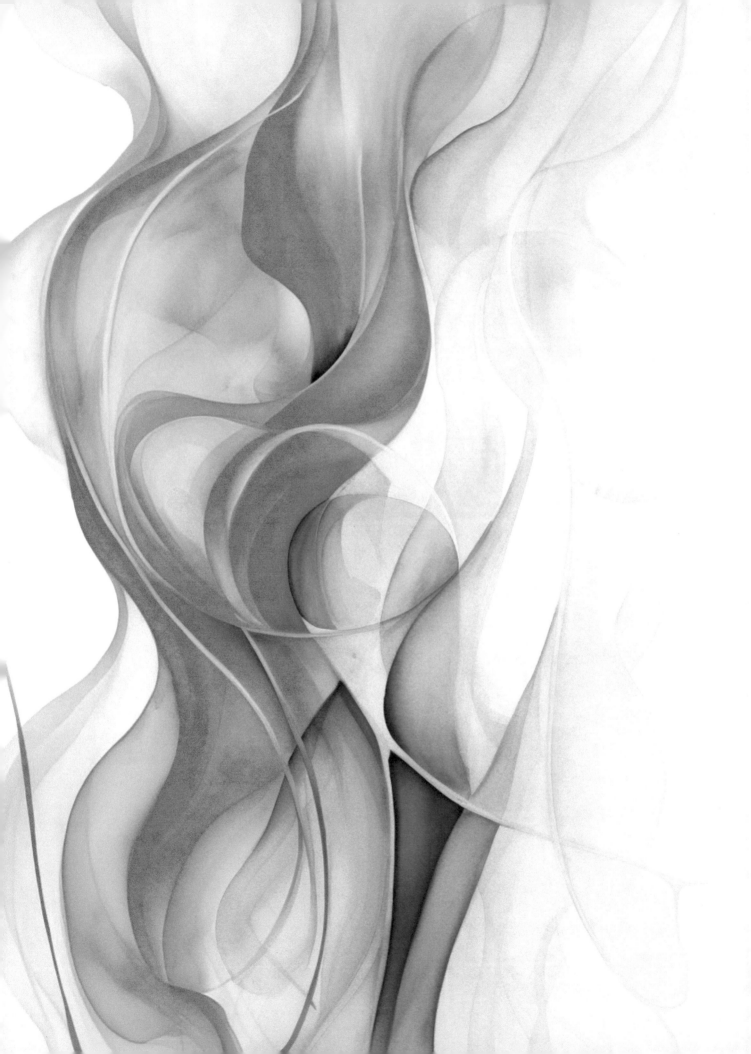

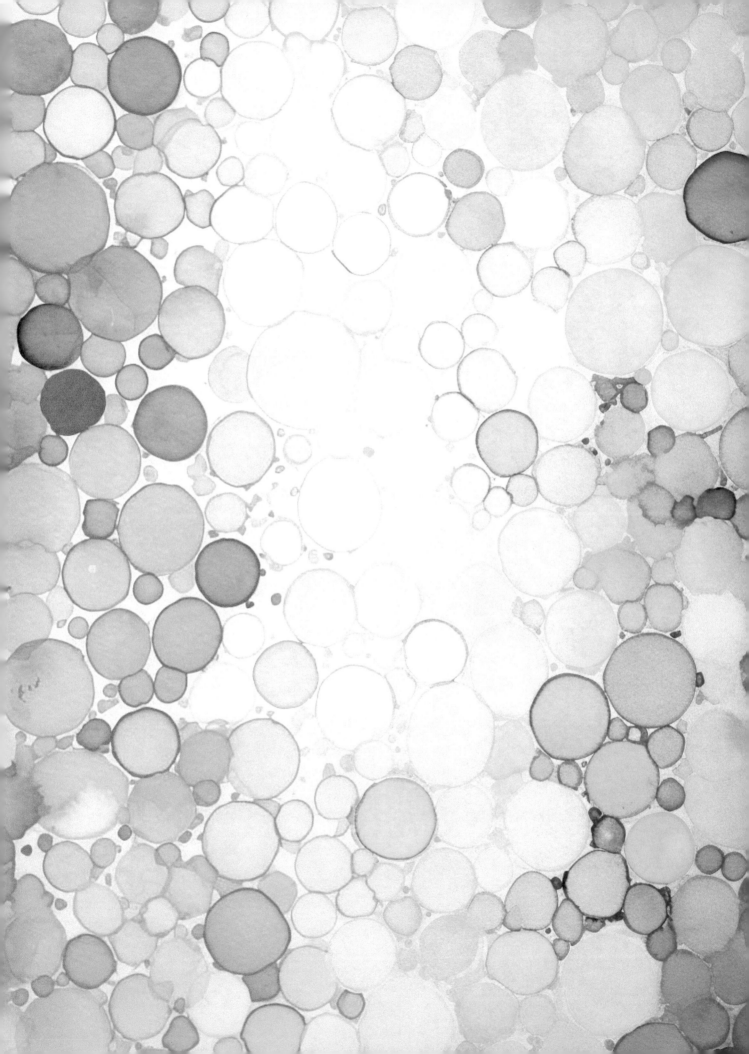

Thank you

We greatly appreciate the time you've dedicated to this book. It has been a true pleasure and honor to share this journey with you. That's why, if you have 30 seconds, we would love to read your impressions about this book on Amazon.

Your feedback helps others discover this book. Scan this code and share your thoughts and opinions.

To leave your review:
1. Open the camera on your mobile device.
2. Point your mobile device's camera at the QR code below.
3. The page to leave your review will appear in your browser.

AMAZON.COM

AMAZON.CO.UK

Thank you for your time and support.

Made in the USA
Columbia, SC
07 December 2024

48692487R00041